FLOOD RESPONSE TEAMS

I0877844

BY EMMA KAISER

WWW.APEXEDITIONS.COM

Copyright © 2025 by Apex Editions, Mendota Heights, MN 55120. All rights reserved. No part of this book may be reproduced or utilized in any form or by any means without written permission from the publisher.

Apex is distributed by North Star Editions:
sales@northstareditions.com | 888-417-0195

Produced for Apex by Red Line Editorial.

Photographs ©: Sue Ogrocki/AP Images, cover; Dana Gray/Caledonian Record/AP Images, 1, 8–9; US Air National Guard/Cover Images/AP Images, 4–5; Shutterstock Images, 6, 7, 10–11, 12, 13, 14–15, 16–17, 29; Peter Gercke/picture-alliance/dpa/AP Images, 18–19; Dan Bates/The Herald/AP Images, 20–21; Arun Sankar K./AP Images, 22–23; Becker & Bredel/picture-alliance/dpa/AP Images, 24–25; James Quigg/The Victor Valley Daily Press/AP Images, 27

Library of Congress Control Number: 2023921624

ISBN
978-1-63738-916-4 (hardcover)
978-1-63738-956-0 (paperback)
979-8-89250-052-4 (ebook pdf)
979-8-89250-014-2 (hosted ebook)

Printed in the United States of America
Mankato, MN
082024

NOTE TO PARENTS AND EDUCATORS

Apex books are designed to build literacy skills in striving readers. Exciting, high-interest content attracts and holds readers' attention. The text is carefully leveled to allow students to achieve success quickly. Additional features, such as bolded glossary words for difficult terms, help build comprehension.

TABLE OF CONTENTS

CHAPTER 1

WATER RESCUE

It is July 2023. Rain falls for days in Vermont. Rivers begin to rise. Large parts of the state flood.

In Montpelier, Vermont, floodwater filled many streets and buildings.

Floods in Vermont damaged more than 4,000 homes.

Water covers roads and washes away bridges. It traps hundreds of people in their homes. The **current** pushes a woman's car off the road. She becomes **stranded**.

FLASH FLOODS

Floods that happen suddenly are called flash floods. They often happen when lots of rain falls in a short amount of time. They are most common in low places near rivers or coasts.

Most flash floods are caused by rain. But some happen when dams break.

Some rescue teams came from other states to help in Vermont.

A flood response team wades through the rushing water. They reach the stranded woman. The team frees her from the car and brings her to safety.

FAST FACT

Flood response teams rescued more than 200 people during the Vermont floods.

CHAPTER 2

DEADLY DISASTERS

Floods are often caused by heavy rain. Some floods happen after **hurricanes**. Tsunamis also cause floods. Their huge waves wash over land near the coast.

Some places got more than 50 inches (127 cm) of rain during Hurricane Harvey.

Just 2 feet (0.6 m) of water can wash away most cars.

Floodwater is very dangerous. It may be more than 30 feet (9 m) deep. And it often flows very quickly. It can sweep away cars, people, and buildings.

LOTS OF DAMAGE

Floods cause many problems. Buildings may lose power. Drinking water may be **polluted**. To stay safe, people often need to leave flooded areas. But floods damage roads. Travel is difficult.

Floodwater is often very dirty. It may carry diseases.

Floods can harm or kill many people. So, flood responders rush to help. They find people and bring them to safety.

FAST FACT

In 1931, a flood in China caused the deaths of more than two million people.

Floodwater can rise quickly. People may be trapped in their homes.

CHAPTER 3

TOOLS AND TRAINING

Flood response teams are often part of local emergency departments. Some people work for their communities. Others are **volunteers**.

Some police officers and firefighters help during floods.

All flood responders go through lots of training. They practice swimming in rough water and finding people at night. They also learn to throw and tie rescue ropes.

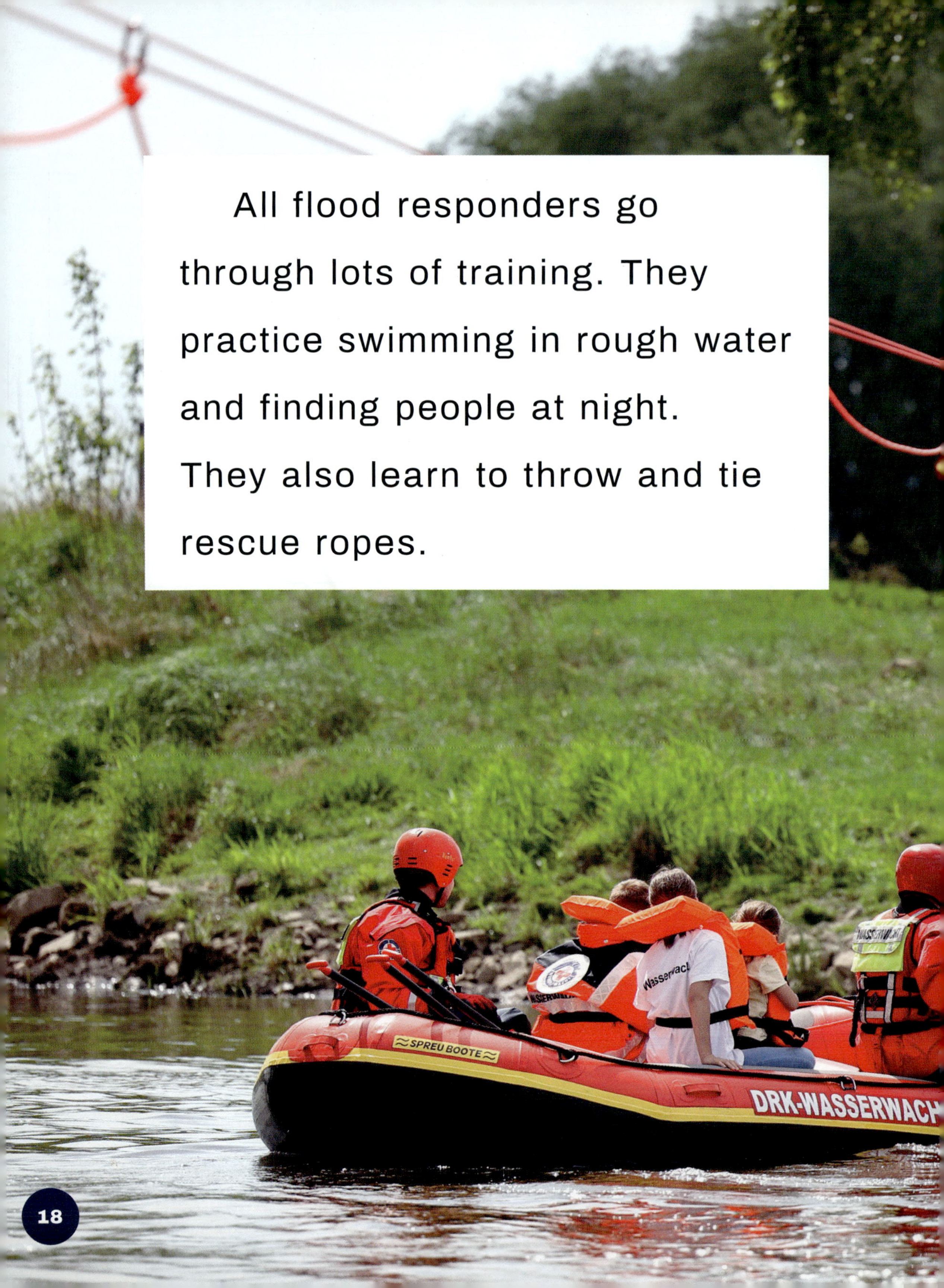

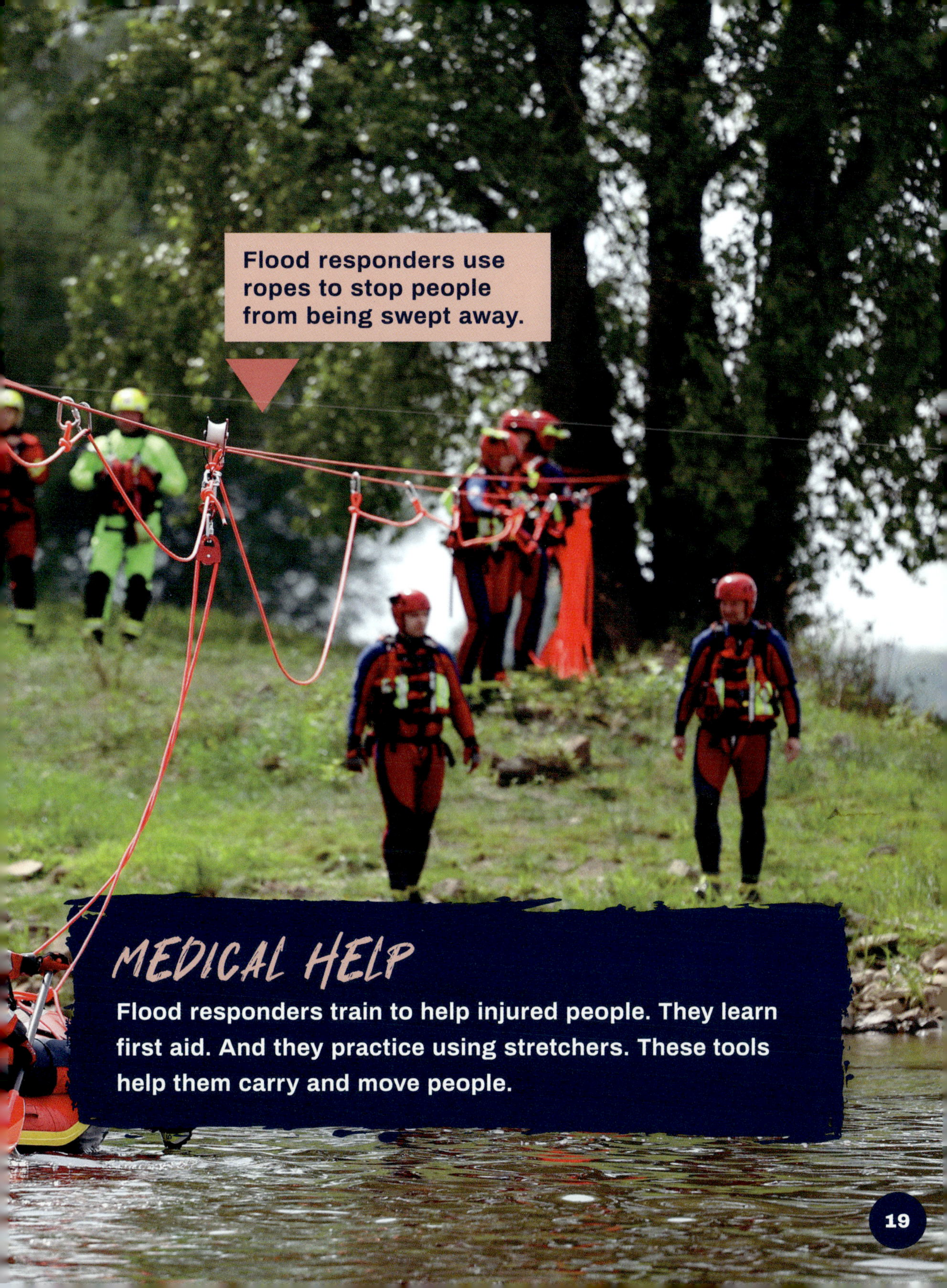

Flood responders use ropes to stop people from being swept away.

MEDICAL HELP

Flood responders train to help injured people. They learn first aid. And they practice using stretchers. These tools help them carry and move people.

Floodwater can be dark and hard to see through.

Many rescues use boats. Floodwater is **unpredictable**. So, responders practice steering in fast or rough water. And they learn to watch out for **debris**.

FAST FACT

Some responders join **elite** teams. They travel to help in many places.

CHAPTER 4

ON THE JOB

Faster responses save more lives. So, teams work as quickly as possible. They use maps to find which areas are flooded. **Dispatchers** may also tell teams where to find people.

Helicopters may fly above flooded areas to help teams find survivors.

To escape surging water, people may go to roofs or upper levels of buildings. Responders check these places. They travel by boat or helicopter.

KEEPING WATCH

Some members of flood response teams may go downstream during rescues. They catch people who fall in the water. Others wait upstream. They watch for large pieces of debris.

Rescue boats can only hold a few passengers. So, response teams often make many trips.

Cars often get stuck on flooded roads. To reach drivers, rescue teams may wade through water. If water is moving too fast, they may use boats or helicopters.

FAST FACT

Some teams use dogs that are trained to find people in water.

Rescue workers may have to break windows to get into cars. ▶

PRO TEC
PRO TEC

COMPREHENSION QUESTIONS

Write your answers on a separate piece of paper.

1. Write a few sentences describing the main ideas of Chapter 2.
2. Would you like to be a part of a flood response team? Why or why not?
3. Where are flash floods more common?
   - **A.** low places near rivers or coasts
   - **B.** low places far from rivers or coasts
   - **C.** high places near farmland
4. What could happen if no one waited downstream during a rescue?
   - **A.** More people could fall into the water.
   - **B.** People who fall into the water could float away.
   - **C.** No one could watch out for debris.

5. What does **dangerous** mean in this book?

Floodwater is very ***dangerous****. It may be more than 30 feet (9 m) deep. And it often flows very quickly.*

A. easy to stop
B. slow moving
C. unsafe

6. What does **surging** mean in this book?

To escape ***surging*** *water, people may go to roofs or upper levels of buildings.*

A. draining away
B. quickly rising
C. slowly cooling

Answer key on page 32.

GLOSSARY

current

A movement of water that goes in a certain way.

debris

Pieces of something that broke or fell apart.

dispatchers

Emergency workers who take phone calls from people who need help.

elite

The best of the best.

hurricanes

Large storms with strong, spinning winds and heavy rain.

polluted

Made dirty or unsafe.

stranded

Stuck in a place and not able to leave.

unpredictable

Hard to guess what will happen.

volunteers

People who help without being paid.

TO LEARN MORE

BOOKS

Becker, Trudy. *2022 Pakistan Floods*. Minneapolis: Mendota Heights, MN: Apex Editions, 2024.

Gagliardi, Sue. *Hurricane Katrina*. Mendota Heights, MN: Focus Readers, 2020.

Pettiford, Rebecca. *Floods*. Minneapolis: Bellwether Media, 2020.

ONLINE RESOURCES

Visit **www.apexeditions.com** to find links and resources related to this title.

ABOUT THE AUTHOR

Emma Kaiser is a writer and educator based in western Minnesota. She has a master of fine arts in creative writing from the University of Minnesota, and her writing has been published in a number of magazines and publications. She is the author of several other nonfiction books for students.

INDEX

ANSWER KEY:
1. Answers will vary; 2. Answers will vary; 3. A; 4. B; 5. C; 6. B